MW00332960

Ten Chosen Women

ISBN 978-1-954095-58-8 (Paperback)
Ten Chosen Women
Copyright © 2021 Jaya Wilkin

All rights reserved.

No part of this publication may be reproduced, distributed, or transmitted in any form or by any means, including photocopying, recording, or other electronic or mechanical methods, without the prior written permission of the publisher, except in the case of brief quotations embodied in critical reviews and certain other noncommercial uses permitted by copyright law.

For permission requests, write to the publisher at the address below.

Yorkshire Publishing
4613 E. 91st St,
Tulsa, OK 74137
www.YorkshirePublishing.com
918.394.2665

Printed in the USA

Ten Chosen Women

Poems and Reflections

Jaya Wilkin

TULSA

For my Aji (grandmother) who once in her small Indian kitchen passed the message of life-changing hope to her daughters, who then told her daughters, and which I passed to my daughters…and so on…and so on.

Jaya Wilkin
Ten Chosen Women

Jaya Wilkin has a Master's degree in TESOL from Biola University and an M.Ed. from Southern Wesleyan University. As a preacher's kid growing up near Toronto, Canada, she attended numerous churches and Christian functions, listening to boring sermons and drawing on visitor cards and offering envelopes placed on the pews in front of her. But Jaya did learn something from hearing various sermons and preachers as she grew up. She learned that God has a plan and purpose for each one of us. She learned about the important characters who faced challenges and struggles but somehow God used them. This book is about pursuing, conquering, and living out His purpose.

AUTHOR'S NOTE

The poems were inspired by my interest in the paternal ancestry of Jesus throughout the Bible. Reading through the long list of fathers, I would notice only a few mothers were mentioned. I read their stories along with those of several other mothers and thought about their unique perspectives from being in Jesus' lineage yet never knowing God's ultimate plan. But what if God somehow did reveal to them their true purpose and what if these Ten Chosen Women felt the need to pass on this message to the next generation?

    I wrote the first ten poems in a similar style to Robert Frost's, *The Road Not Taken*, with four stanzas and the five-line rhyming pattern of ABAAB. The first stanza introduces the character, the second shares their struggles or challenges, the third is where they find hope and strength, and, finally, the fourth stanza reveals their ultimate redemption and joy. The final poem celebrates the generational bond of mothers passing on the message. The poems are accompanied by reflections, Bible readings, questions, and *Did you know* sections. The book can be read as a devotional or in group settings; however in our fast-paced world sometimes it is nice to pause and reflect on a simple poem and its symbolism, allusion, and imagery. Journey along as you soar like doves and connect with these Ten Chosen Women. Here are their stories.

Eve

Under the oak tree, she sits alone
with anguished tears and soaking hair.
Aware of shame, she trembles, she groans,
shattered heart with aching moans.
Flourishing garden in disrepair.

There were never thoughts of wanting more,
her life, pure bliss, consuming love.
But the tempting voice beguiled her core,
promising wisdom doomed to war.
Destruction, separation, cursed from above.

The only hope within her soul,
a promise above so undeserved.
A future child, his hand to hold,
leading the world out of shadows and cold.
Light of life ending darkness on earth.

So, standing strong, she faces the storm,
through years passing by with offspring dissension.
She raises aged hands wrinkled and worn,
and cries aloud a son will be born!
While the dove soars high along the horizon.

Adam lay with his wife again and she gave
birth to a son and named him Seth...
Genesis 4:25-26

Read Genesis Chapter 3

The Bible is a true historical story. It is not fiction or the fairy tale stories we learned in Sunday school. I wrote the poem *Eve* to reveal our powerful historical roots through the very first woman created. I wanted to share how God's message of hope might have been carried on by our first mother—Eve. Can you imagine living in a pain-free, extremely content, blissful, peaceful world, to suddenly feeling physical pain, emotional pain, and social anguish? She must have felt utter hopelessness.

"And I will put enmity between you and the woman,
and between your offspring and hers; he will crush your
head, and you will strike his heel." Genesis 3:15

However, the good news is that God's story does not end with the problem of destruction and curse throughout the earth. God gives us a clue by telling Eve that someone—her own offspring—will restore the earth and mankind one day. Throughout the Bible, we can follow this journey of figuring out the puzzle of who *he* is. Our mother Eve had hope and I believe her purpose was to pass on this message to her children and her children's children. We also can share in the same hope as we read His story and learn who this Redeemer really is through these special women.

Discussion Questions:

1. Describe Eve's poem in one word and share why you chose that word.

2. Why is Eve in anguish and alone at the beginning of the poem?

3. Why did Eve eat the forbidden fruit when she had everything she needed?

4. In Eve's poem, she is overwhelmed with guilt and shame for betraying God. What is the hope she holds on to?

5. The poem moves from darkness and storm to finally a glimmer of light. When have you felt darkness in your life, and have you ever experienced the hope and light like Eve?

Did you know?

In questioning its accuracy, there is no other ancient literature, so well attested, by so many manuscripts, over such a length of time, as the Christian Bible. Christians can take the entire Bible in their hands and say with confidence that they hold the true word of God, handed down from generation to generation throughout the centuries. The outstanding scholar F.F. Bruce concluded that the evidence from the *Dead Sea Scrolls* confirms what we already had good reason to believe: "The Jewish scribes of the early Christian centuries copied and recopied the text of the Hebrew Bible with the utmost fidelity" (Bruce [1956] 2006, 62.)

Naamah

In silence, she stood and watched them mock
her husband's seemingly failed approach.
A call from above to build an ark,
it came to her as an after-shock
that the world may flood, yet she should float.

All coupled creatures found their way
in quiet formation marching aboard.
In awe and wonder, no distraction by rain,
drowned out the mockers while her family shut in.
And drifted swiftly as harsh waters rose.

Long days and nights she kept them sane
through singing and laughing and keeping them fed.
Hiding uncertainty, her fear and pain,
yet the dove did return, promising change.
Finding purpose, calm waters, looking ahead.

Then waters receded, they opened the doors,
as blinding light flooded a promising world.
The rainbow reminder destruction no more,
her inner heart calmed, as countless doves soar.
And she passes the message with maternal words.

*Then God said to Noah, "Come out of the ark, you
and your wife and your sons and their wives."*
Genesis 8:15-16

Read Genesis Chapters 6-9

The name of Noah's wife is not mentioned in the Bible but several sources, including the Jewish writing known as the *Genesis Rabba* (c.5th Century AD), suggest that Naamah, who is mentioned in Genesis 4:22, was Noah's wife. I had never been able to identify with Naamah until I tried to place myself in her situation. I wonder if she tried to stay outwardly positive while she felt deep fear and uncertainty. She must have asked herself: How long will it remain like this? Will supplies run out? Will we have enough food?

During the recent Global Pandemic, I watched people around us hoarding basic necessities and others mocking our realities. I find that I feel an unexplainable inner peace that Naamah may have also shared. Her peace was knowing that a Savior would someday come from her offspring. My peace is knowing that He did come and that He will return once more to save us all.

*I have set my rainbow in the clouds, and it will be the sign
of the covenant between me and the earth.* Genesis 9:13

The modern-day symbol of the rainbow can be found in fairy-tale unicorns, clothing, and waving flags, yet I challenge us all again to read the story of God's covenant with Noah and be reminded that we have the peace and comfort of knowing God will never destroy all living creatures. Our mother Naamah knew of the promise and passed it to her offspring; hopefully, we can take comfort in this when we face hardships in our own lives.

Discussion Questions:

1. Describe Naamah's poem in one word and share why you chose that word.

2. The poem is a unique perspective on Noah's wife. Describe what her character might have been like.

3. If God is so loving, why would He flood the earth and destroy His creation?

4. How must Naamah have felt when everyone mocked her husband? Have you ever had to protect your children or loved ones in the same way?

5. In Naamah's poem, we find a mother who must remain calm in the midst of a storm outside the ark. Can you think of a time when you had to hide your true feelings from your children or loved ones?

6. Naamah had to put her faith and trust in a seemingly impossible plan. When have you had to put your trust in God even though the future seemed bleak? Were you able to see the light at the end of the "rainbow"?

Did you know?

There is evidence that the Flood really did happen. One proof is that no one can explain the billions of fossils in mass graves. Vast numbers of animals were buried and fossilized so quickly that some could not even finish swallowing their meals, while other animals were in the middle of giving birth. The evidence of tree trunks standing upright can also be explained by a quick burial. The same kind of rock layer can be found on multiple continents, suggesting a global flood. These rock layers found on the earth are bent, not broken, suggesting that the Flood laid these layers rapidly and the rocks were bent before they could dry out and harden. (*The Flood*, 2019.)

Sarah

Pharaohs and Kings stunned by her beauty,
causing her fear to pose as a sibling.
But she knew in her heart God's promise of mercy
would make them a nation as night stars of plenty.
Following, trusting, still childless and aging.

Impatient, she takes control of God's plan
and forces another to bear them a child.
Envious, angry, she watches small hand
held by her husband, fueled by demands.
Regretting, still barren, unreconciled.

Then He appeared and revealed what was promised
while she hid and listened, doubting and laughing.
Her giving birth was something amiss,
a frail old woman, she had to dismiss.
But looking above, she saw the dove soaring.

At last in old age they had a son
and she laughed and nursed, while body still swollen.
Years later she smiled as she breathed her last one
while she held her child's hand before setting sun.
Keeping the promise, she entered the heavens.

He took him outside and said, "Look up at the heavens and count the stars—if indeed you can count them…so shall your offspring be."
Genesis 15:5

Read Genesis 18:1-15 and Genesis 20-21:1-7

I think of Sarah as a very complex character. Outwardly, she was extremely beautiful, so much so that her husband told her to pretend she was his sister to spare their lives from important leaders. I wonder if she was angry with her husband for having to play along and give herself to another man. Or was she okay with his scheme because she knew God's ultimate plan to have children as numerous as the stars—one of them being the Savior? As she got older, she became impatient and tried to manipulate God's plan by forcing her husband to have a child with her maidservant. I think we can all identify with wanting to be in control and not having the patience to wait on Him. In 2000, God revealed His glory and purpose to me one fall night and my faith has never been shaken since. However, twenty years later, I am still waiting and wondering what my real purpose is in this life and will I be patient enough to wait on Him.

God has brought me laughter, and everyone who hears about this will laugh with me.
Genesis 21:6

When Sarah finally learned she would be a mother, she laughed, not believing it could happen in her old age and she laughed out of joy when it did. God's sense of humor reveals that everything happens in His timing. Unfortunately, Sarah never lived to meet her son's wife and her future grandchildren, but I am sure she knew the importance of passing on the message of hope from mother Eve, as she lived out her days in joy and laughter. Take comfort in knowing we can do the same when we let go and let God!

Discussion Questions:

1. Describe Sarah's poem in one word and explain.

2. God promised that Abraham's descendants would be as numerous as the stars, yet Sarah was impatient and tried to take the future into her own hands. What is the consequence of impatience and not waiting on God's timing?

3. Why did Sarah laugh?

4. Have you ever laughed at a plan you thought was impossible in your life?

5. Sarah posed as her husband's sister for safety without trusting in God's protection. Have you ever tried to hide your true character? What were the consequences of trying to be someone else?

Did you know?

The cave where Sarah was buried, known as Machpelah, is located in Jerusalem and is still intact today. The beautiful structure resembles a temple, with six monumental tombs commemorating the patriarchs and matriarchs. In the twentieth century, a young girl was lowered into the underground room to investigate. There she found a staircase leading to a long hallway and tomb area. People today describe their visit to Machpelah cave as a holy spiritually uplifting experience. (Kaiser Jr. and Garrett [2005] 2010, 172.)

Rebekah

On that day as usual she went to draw water
while his servant waited to ask for a drink.
With no hesitation she sealed her own future,
receiving God's purpose and telling her father,
"I will go" and she left them, accepting his ring.

As husband and wife, they traveled afar,
her captivating beauty and fear for his life,
feigning identity under her scarf.
Fulfilling her purpose so numerous as stars,
disguise did not hide his love for his wife.

At last, it was time she would be a mother,
two babies, two nations within her womb.
One brother stronger compared to the other,
yet he would be one to serve under the younger.
Family line to the Savior, the other to gloom.

Her boys grew up, one rugged and strong,
other mild-mannered, meek disposition.
And she knew in her heart as she looked to the dove,
her preferential blessing, even if she was wrong,
would go to the youngest, the next generation.

And they blessed Rebekah and said to her "…
may you increase to thousands upon thousands; may
your offspring possess the gates of their enemies."
Genesis 24:60

Read Genesis 24, Genesis 25:19-34, and Genesis 27:5-10

I think for some it is difficult to understand Rebekah's conflicting characteristics. On the one hand, she is seen as a noble young woman who immediately leaves her beloved family to marry a stranger in order to fulfill God's purpose. When she meets her husband Isaac, she is quickly drawn to his quiet devotion to God. Later, her favoritism towards her younger son Jacob rather than Esau leads to deceiving her husband, leaving us a little confused.

…Esau said, "What good is the birthright to me?" Genesis 25:32

However, we should not be quick to conclude that Rebekah chose only one son to love and wished only for him to have the blessing. She knew God's purpose for Jacob while he was in her womb. She was aware of Esau's dismissal of the importance of his birthright because he chose to marry ungodly wives. She knew the significance of passing on Eve's message of hope for a Savior. I wish we could rewrite the ending of her story but we all can identify with not trusting when God is in control. She should have remembered that Jacob receiving his humanly father's blessing was nothing compared to receiving the blessings from his heavenly father. Even though Rebekah's story ends negatively, we can take solace in knowing her sacrifice of leaving the comforts of her home to fulfill God's promise is greatly to be revered.

Discussion Questions:

1. Describe Rebekah's poem in one word and explain why you chose that word.

2. Compare young Rebekah's character to the older Rebekah. How was she the same? What changed about her as she matured?

3. Rebekah decided to leave everything and join Isaac's servant for a new life. Have you ever taken a risk because you believed it was the right thing to do?

4. Did Rebekah favor one son over the other? Was this part of God's plan?

5. Just like his father, Isaac pretended Rebekah was his sister instead of his wife because he was afraid. Why do you think he made the same mistake as his father? Why do we have a hard time trusting in God's protection?

Did you know?

The authorship of the first books of the Bible is attributed to Moses. The question is: How accurate is Genesis if Moses was born many years later? Some Christians believe in the inerrancy of the Scripture given to Moses directly through the Holy Spirit. Others argue that Moses relied on eyewitness records from Adam, Noah, Abraham, and Jacob possibly written on clay tablets. Moses may have compiled the stories into one book crediting him as the author. Most important, though, is that we can trust God in His word that the stories we read are His stories. (Strobel 2010, 42.)

Leah

As oldest daughter, arranged to marry
a man who had eyes for only one other.
A burden to bear she had to carry,
born with plain features that held no beauty,
he chose the sister, not older but younger.

For seven years he served them well,
patiently waiting for young sibling's hand.
Wedding day came, promises not kept,
blinding vows, switching places, weakened eyes wept,
betrayed, he continued to work their land.

And when God saw she was not loved,
opening her womb, he gave her a son.
Hoping and praying he would not lose sight of,
more children to come, a gift from above.
Perpetual rejection of her true devotion.

Finally revealing her one true purpose,
from her would come the saving lion.
Tethering his colt to the choicest branches,
at last, true love, shown through his blessings.
Doves cry no more under setting sun.

*She conceived again, and when she gave birth
to a son she said, "Because the Lord heard that
I am not loved, he gave me this one..."*
Genesis 29:33

Genesis 29:14-35, and Genesis 49:8-12

Leah's life story is a sad one. Up until this point, Jesus' mothers are described as being very beautiful, but Leah is described as having weak eyes and being unattractive to her husband. She must have felt unloved and undesirable. For fourteen years, her husband Jacob worked her father's land to earn not hers but her younger sister's hand in marriage. The Bible says that Jacob loved Rachel more than Leah. My heart aches when I read that each time she gave birth, she yearned for her husband's love and attention. When Jacob blesses his twelve sons, it is her son Judah who is greatly to be honored and praised. He is the one who will carry on the promise of the Messiah coming through her lineage. God gave Leah special priority and used her for His purpose.

*There Abraham and his wife Sarah were buried, there Isaac and his
wife Rebekah were buried, and there I buried Leah.* Genesis 49:31

After Leah gives birth to six sons and one daughter, she is not mentioned again until Jacob's dying instructions, when we learn she was buried in a special place with his family members. I would like to think that near the end of their lives, Jacob did honor, love, and respect her as she deserved. Leah teaches us that it is not outward appearances or approval from others that holds importance, but the love and blessings that only come from God give us true worth.

Discussion Questions:

1. Describe Leah's poem in one word. Why did you choose that word?

2. How are the two sisters different?

3. God chose Leah, the unlikely sister, to be part of Jesus' ancestral line. What does this say about who God chooses?

4. Do you think there was sibling rivalry between the two sisters? Leah may have had a difficult life competing with Rachel, but she was buried in a place of honor. When you face struggles on earth where can you find the real reward?

5. Jacob loved Rachel and later favored her sons Joseph and Benjamin over the other ten brothers. Compare the twelve blessings from Jacob in Genesis 49:1-28. Who was given positive blessings? Who was given short or even negative blessings? What might be the reason for this?

Did you know?

It is possible that a marriage could take place without ever seeing the bride. In those days, the newly married wife would have worn a veil to cover her face. When the consummation of Jacob and Leah's marriage occurred alone at night, the darkness and possibly wine from the wedding could have blurred Jacob's vision. Despite not knowing the exact details, we can conclude that several scenarios could have hidden Leah's identity from Jacob. (Strobel 2010, 48.)

Tamar

She lingers and watches drenched palms in sway,
young and strong, rain cannot break.
Alone, twice widowed, she can only pray
for a child to redeem her unfortunate state.
Dishonest plan to relieve heartache.

In quiet, she waits as palm leaves still,
temptress disguise, she beckons towards
hastening the deal while using her skill.
Soon child inside, the promise fulfilled;
Binding through word, a seal, and a cord.

Angry trees thrash and bend in storm
as mask uncovers and truth revealed.
Her punishment death, they run to swarm
but through grace and mercy, she is transformed
because of God's promise to strike his heel.

Twin palms stand tall through gentle breezes,
blessings abound for not one child but two.
Seemingly strong, one stretches and reaches
but the second breaks out, bursting doves, unceasing.
Hope is not lost, the message continues.

Judah recognized them and said, "She is more righteous
than I, since I wouldn't give her to my son Shelah."
Genesis 38:26

Read Genesis 38

Tamar means palm tree. Living here in the south, I am amazed by so many beautiful palms growing both naturally and flourishing in residential areas. I know that most of the trees here in my neighborhood were intentionally planted because they are exactly positioned to give us the best esthetic view. When I read the story of Judah and Tamar, I wonder why God placed this strange story in the midst of one other captivating story about Joseph (Judah's brother). However, when you look deeper, you realize God's great purpose in using Tamar to fulfill His promise of the coming Messiah. Did Tamar recognize the importance of carrying on Judah's line through words of wisdom from her grandmother-in-law Leah? I am awed that she went to such great lengths, dressing as a prostitute, jeopardizing her reputation and almost facing punishment by death to accomplish her mission of having a child for God's purpose.

Judah, the father of Perez and Zerah, whose
mother was Tamar. Matthew 1:3

Incredibly, Tamar is given recognition years later in the book of Matthew. In a time when genealogies did not normally contain even a single female name, there her name is included. Her son Perez, which means "breaking out," is a reminder that we all should break out of our comfort zones and tell others of God's compassion and redemption for our imperfections and sin. If God can use someone like Tamar, then He will certainly use us to fulfill His perfect plan.

Discussion Questions:

1. Describe Tamar's poem in one word and share why you chose that word.

2. How does the image of the palm trees compare to Tamar's life?

3. Why was Tamar so desperate to have a child?

4. Did Tamar do the right thing or was she deceptive? If this was God's purpose, what could have been an alternate way for her to carry on the line?

5. Have you ever taken things into your own hands instead of waiting on God?

6. Why did Judah say, "She is more righteous than I?"

Did you know?

Before writing was invented, seals were a way of signing important documents. It was made with a hard substance such as stone or metal and made into a ring or worn around the neck. The unique stamp would leave a design or impression marking the owner's identity. The cord was like a rope that binds things together and is used by a person of authority. The staff was carved with ornamental design and used for walking but it also represented power. When Judah gave his seal, cord, and staff to Tamar, he was also giving up his identity, authority, and power. ("Genesis - What Is the Significance of Seal, Cord, and Staff?" n.d.)

Rahab

Shadows on walls, candlelight dims,
her body used as reflection of guilt.
And once again she lets the men in
but her candle blows out by sudden wind.
A change in her heart that softens and melts.

As these men bring hope and light from above,
her new faith shields them by protecting with lies.
Hiding them safe, then releasing like doves,
she showed them kindness through innocent love,
from enemy walls to peaceful allies.

War trumpets sound, surrounded by all,
her fear diminished by hanging scarlet cord.
Loud shouts of terror, outside city falls,
yet faith never wavers and strengthens inner walls.
Her family protected, not one death by sword.

As years go on and old life forgotten,
married, new home, respectable life.
And who would believe the promise given,
hope would come from one of her children.
Walls broken down and in comes the light.

"...I know that the Lord has given this land to
you and that a great fear of you has fallen on us, so
that all...are melting in fear because of you."
Joshua 2:9

Read Joshua 2

Rahab was a prostitute whose house was built in the city wall.
The Israelites were about to invade and attack her city and take over
her land. She knew how powerful the Israelite God was and her heart
melted not only in fear but in awe of Him. She must have sensed that
these men were different from the regular customers who entered her
home. While she was used to men taking advantage of her body, they
only asked for refuge and safety. She made the quick decision to hide
them up on her roof. What amazing faith she had to risk her life for
strangers.

But Joshua spared Rahab the prostitute, with her family
and all who belonged to her, because she hid the men...and
she lives among the Israelites to this day." Joshua 6:25

For her kindness, she was promised that her life and all her
household would be spared. All she had to do was hang a scarlet cord
in her window and persuade her whole family to stay within the walls
of her house. How difficult it must have been to convince her family
she had changed and also to put their trust in her. I wonder if she had
a face-to-face encounter with God because, not only did her heart
melt, but she was truly a new person from the inside out.

The good news is that all their lives were saved because of
Rahab. She eventually married an Israelite named Salmon and lived
a reputable life as one of the patriarch grandmothers of the greatest
kings who lived, David. In fact, she is later mentioned a few times in

the New Testament as being a strong woman of faith (Hebrews 11:31 and James 2:25). God not only changed Rahab's total life direction but He also used her for His ultimate plan of redemption.

Discussion Questions:

1. Give one word to describe Rahab's poem. Give your reason why you chose this word.

2. Describe how Rahab's life changed after the spies came to her home.

3. Was it right for Rahab to lie? Is it morally okay to lie to protect others?

4. Rahab and her family must have been extremely frightened when the walls were coming down around them. What a relief they must have felt to be saved. Has fear ever "fallen" on you? How did you find relief or comfort?

5. God used Rahab, a former prostitute for His great purpose. Do you believe He can use anyone? Have you ever witnessed someone who completely changed?

Did you know?

There is evidence that Rahab and her family escaped death. Excavations have proven that an earthquake or powerful tremor occurred during the fall of the city of Jericho. But what about Rahab's house, which was supposedly built in this wall? How did she and her family survive? From 1907 to 1909, archeologists uncovered portions of the city wall still intact with housing built between the lower and upper wall. The house also had lower windows which could have been used for the spies to escape. Archeological evidence is another proof we can trust in the preservation of Rahab and her important family lineage. (Kaiser Jr. and Garrett [2005] 2010, 975.)

Ruth

With aching heart, tears river down,
she clings to her cloak like mother and child.
Choosing the path to foreign town,
planting her feet on new solid ground,
bonded through ties she cannot let die.

Together she takes the old woman's hand,
protecting, providing, and keeping her strong.
As hard-working servant, she gleans the land
while from a distance there stands a man
who thinks in his mind she doesn't belong.

And day by day she gathers the grain
yet her heart knows he must be the one.
So unselfish courage she goes down and lays
her heart proposal, hoping for change.
Matrimony promised before rising sun.

Soon a child clings to grandmother's lap,
soft blanket beats like white breasts of dove.
She ponders how she from faraway land
was given new hope to fulfill the plan.
So legacy lives through both mothers' love.

At this they wept again. Then Orpah kissed her
mother-in-law good-by, but Ruth clung to her."
Ruth 1:14

Read Ruth 1-4

Ruth, meaning "friendship," was a foreigner from a land called Moab who marries into an Israelite family. Moabites were known to worship pagan gods through grotesque and despicable acts. The story of Ruth is one of great redemption and transformation. Her mother-in-law Naomi, a childless widower, tells her daughters-in-law to go back to their homes since she has nothing to offer them. But Ruth decides to stay with her because of their strong bond, and most importantly she chooses to cling to the faith she has in the Israelite God, "Yahweh." Ruth shows extreme unselfish sacrificial love by leaving her homeland and caring and providing for her aged mother-in-law through hard and strenuous labor. Through God's providence, she meets Boaz, a descendant from the line of Judah, whom she bravely proposes to and eventually marries. Thus, she is the one who carries on this important family line of the coming Messiah.

"...May the Lord make the woman who is coming into your
home like Rachel and Leah, who together built up the house
of Israel. May you...be famous in Bethlehem." Ruth 4:11

My own Indian family ancestry has a history of Hindu religious followers, but it was my great-great-grandparents from both sides who made the brave decision, like Ruth, to leave their family traditions and beliefs to worship the Christian God—the same Israelite God of Naomi. How awesome that Ruth, a stranger and foreigner, was used by God to carry on the lineage of the promised Savior. At the end of this story, her husband Boaz and Naomi are especially honored and praised but notice that it is Ruth who is given the greatest recognition by making her name the title of this book. God does not see race, ethnicity, or religious family background as a hindrance to His purpose. All we must do is cling!

Discussion Questions:

1. Give one word to describe Ruth's poem. Why did you choose this word?

2. Why did Naomi tell her daughters in-law to leave? Why did Ruth stay and cling to her?

3. Have you ever traveled to a foreign land or been to an unfamiliar place? What was difficult about your experience? Where did you find comfort—if any?

4. Ruth could have been harmed while she was working hard in the fields. However, she found determination and strength and eventual protection from Boaz. Where does your strength come from in times of difficulty?

5. Why do you think an entire book is written about Ruth? Why is her story important?

Did you know?

In Hebrew tradition, uncovering a man's feet and lying next to him was a non-verbal proposal. Since Boaz was one of Ruth's kinsman-redeemer (a close relative responsible for her), Naomi suggested that Ruth should request marriage. He responded kindly by referencing her as a "woman of noble character" (Ruth 3:11) and made sure the other kinsmen-redeemer passed his property rights legally to him. Ruth acted boldly and Boaz proved to truly be her Redeemer. (Strobel 2010, 363.)

Bathsheba

Immersing within pure floral waters,
over rooftop she catches his watchful eye.
True soldier's wife and military daughter
yet forbidden love she lets him linger.
Deceit cannot hide the child inside.

Pools overflow, drowning in shame,
streaming down tears left broken-hearted.
Innocent husband brought to the grave,
impulsive encounter, undignified name.
Instant royalty, yet not what she wanted.

In anguish, she cries, "please comfort me,"
she watches her child breathing his last.
Yet hope still anchors in raging sea,
a new son is promised, she bows to her knees
as roof doves fly over, storm finally passed.

Waters flow freely from fountains delight,
her wise son established as king of the throne.
Honorable mother, she sits on his right,
never forgetting her Redeemer of light.
The oath still established and written in stone.

*... The woman was very beautiful, and David sent someone
to find out about her. The man said, "Isn't this Bathsheba,
the daughter of Eliam and the wife of Uriah...?"*
2 Samuel 11:2-3

Read 2 Samuel 11 and 1 Kings 1:28-31

Unfortunately, when we think of Bathsheba and her name, we conjure up images of bathing and lustful sin. How ironic that her name means *oath* or promise. Before her encounter with King David, she was a reputable daughter, spouse, and sister to distinct men in David's army. Some people like to speculate that she seduced David by purposely bathing in the open air. Others think that, in her innocence, the powerful King forced her into a relationship. All we can conclude is that her life drastically changed soon afterward. She had to bear the same weight of sin's consequences by losing her innocent husband and enduring the eventual death of her newborn son. Sadly, her new unwanted royal fame, won through an adulterous affair, must have brought shame to her prominent military family.

*When Bathsheba went to King Solomon... [he] bowed down
to her... He had a throne brought for the king's mother,
and she sat down at his right hand.* 1 Kings 2:19

We cannot underestimate the fullness of God's love and total forgiveness for sin. She is redeemed through her new son, Solomon, whom God loved. Consequently, it is her child who is chosen to rule the kingdom and he is known to be the wisest man that ever lived. Some believe that when he wrote about the righteous teachings from a mother in Proverbs 31, he was writing about his own mother. We should not look down on Bathsheba for her unfaithful past but put her on a pedestal, along with the other strong mothers who carried the oath to continue God's teachings and promises of a Savior through their family line.

Discussion Question:

1. What is your one-word reaction to Bathsheba's poem and give an explanation.

2. Bathsheba was bathing for her monthly ceremonial cleansing. As you read the scripture and poem what kinds of emotions might she have had about her encounter with King David?

3. Was Bathsheba innocent of the adulterous act or was she also to blame?

4. Both David and Bathsheba suffered from the loss of their child. Have you ever had to recover from a tragic loss? What are some ways that helped you get through?

5. David and Bathsheba were redeemed through their second son, King Solomon. Think of ways God has redeemed you from making bad choices in the past.

Did you know?

Some people wonder how a loving God could allow innocent children to die. However, some would claim that, if God created life, then He also has the right to take it. God is just, loving and righteous and in Isaiah 7:16, the Bible refers to a time before a child knows right from wrong. After the death of King David's son, he expresses joy in knowing that someday he would join his baby in heaven. We can take comfort in sharing in David's assurance. (Strobel [2010] 2014, 169.)

Mary

Illuminating light, she awakens in fear,
untouched yet chosen to be the one.
New young mother streaming down tears,
bearing disgrace yet all made clear,
leaping for joy for what is to come.

Betrothed to marry in Judah's line,
humble beginnings for babe inside.
Giving birth on soil near animal cries,
heaven celebrates with brilliant skies,
Eve's Deliverer has finally arrived.

Marveling at this child of wonder,
giving instruction while He taught love.
His wisdom exploding a voice like no other,
astonishing crowds with extraordinary power.
Son dazzling bright like descending doves.

Proudly she watched His growing fame,
His love shined for all, but others sought
to end the light and darken His name.
Yet final breath meant lasting flame,
she continued His fire, still lit in heart.

You will be with child and give birth to a son, and
you are to give him the name Jesus. He will be great
and will be called the Son of the Most High...
Luke 1:31-32

Read Luke 1:26-2:52

Mary is the final and most revered mother of the ten. The long-awaited anticipation of a Savior is revealed through Mary's son Jesus. He would be born of a virgin in Bethlehem in the line of Judah. The chance of this is so remarkable that we cannot dismiss it as being mere coincidence. Mary knew of the hope of a Savior through her family's Jewish teachings, yet it must have surprised her to realize she would be the one chosen to deliver him. Imagine a young unmarried virgin facing the embarrassment of being with child, giving birth in an animal stall, and then trying to raise this Child of God. I wonder how difficult it must have been to discipline Him as a mother, yet at the same time, He was also her Lord who astonished crowds with His teachings and miracles. What is most heart-wrenching was having to watch her innocent Son endure horrific punishment and excruciating death on a cross. She must have wondered whether He really was the promised Savior as she saw Him take His last breath.

They all joined together constantly in prayer, along with the women
and Mary the mother of Jesus, and with his brothers. Acts 1:14

Fortunately, the story does not end there. Jesus miraculously returned from the dead and appeared to over 500 witnesses. Because of this, Mary became a fiery prayer warrior and eyewitness to all her Son accomplished. Eve's promise of a Deliverer amazingly passed on through the offspring of significant mothers and was finally fulfilled through Mary. Like these women, we all face trials, we all are imperfect, but we have assurance that God can still use us to fulfill His promises. We all can share in Eve's hope of a promised Deliverer.

Discussion Questions:

1. Give your reaction to Mary's poem in one word. Why did you choose this word?

2. Discuss your teenage years. How do they compare with Mary's. What kind of load and responsibility did she bear?

3. Mary had to helplessly watch her son die. Have you ever experienced a loss and felt helpless?

4. The Bible says that Mary pondered these things in her heart. What does this mean? Do you think she knew He was the Messiah?

5. Describe how Mary must have felt to reunite with her Son after His Resurrection. What do you think she did right after witnessing Him alive? What would you do?

Did you know?

There are over 300 prophesies of the coming Messiah in the Old Testament. The book of Isaiah writes about being born of a virgin and performing miracles. Zechariah talks about his arrival on a donkey, being forsaken and being pierced. Micah remarkably predicts the Messiah's exact birthplace, Bethlehem. Against astronomical odds, only one Person matched these prophetic fingerprints that were written hundreds of years before His birth. Skeptics argue that the Gospel writers fabricated the details to look like Jesus fulfilled them, yet the Jewish community and Christian community living at that time would have easily tried to discredit or make sure what was written really did happen. When one studies the Old Testament thoroughly, we must conclude that only one Person in history matched the deity of the true Messiah and that is Jesus Christ (Strobel 2016, 239–40)

The Mothers of Jesus

Eve's selfish choice lead to the darkness
yet grace from above came a promised son.
Naamah carried on through wind and storm,
then floodwaters receded as doves returned.
Hope passed on to next generation.

Sarah laughed in disbelief
from possible birth in such old age.
Rebekah left her family behind
to raise two nations, saving mankind.
Patience passed on to next generation.

Leah unloved and forever second
yet her son received the best of blessings.
Tamar shunned from shameful disguise
but forgiveness and mercy her twins arrived.
Strength passed on to next generation.

Rahab changed as she opened her home,
walls breaking down, she found her worth.
Ruth clung on with all her might,
risking much to share in the light.
Courage passed on to next generation.

Bathsheba mourned for death of first son
but no one compared to Solomon's wisdom.
Mary was chosen for most difficult task,
to raise the One to fulfill the plan.
Redemption passed on to Our generation.

*We did not follow cleverly invented stories when we
told you about the power and coming of our Lord Jesus
Christ, but we were eyewitnesses of his majesty.*
2 Peter 1:16

Read Matthew 1:1-17

*Eve the mother of Seth…Naamah the mother of Shem…
Sarah the mother of Isaac…Rebekah the mother of Jacob…
Leah the mother of Judah…Tamar the mother of Perez…
Rahab the mother of Boaz…Ruth the mother of Obed…
Bathsheba the mother of Solomon…Mary the mother of Jesus.*

The Bible is not just a book of fiction or mysticism, but a book of historical truths. The stories of these ten mothers all foreshadow the Redeemer who is to come from their ancestry. Jesus fulfilled God's promise: *For God so loved the world that he gave his one and only Son, that whoever believes in him shall not perish but have eternal life.* (John 3:16). The entire Bible points to Jesus as the Savior and the mothers play important roles in fulfilling God's plan. From them, we learn to have hope when we face our struggles. We build patience to endure pain and heartache. We can take courage to do what is right amidst a fallen world. And we know we will win because their Son and our Lord Jesus died on the cross for our sins, overcame death, and was seen alive. Now we can share in God's redemptive almighty power and spend eternity with Him.

Discussion Questions:

1. What are your thoughts on the final poem about Jesus' mothers?

2. Describe each mother's struggles and how she found hope and redemption.

3. Which women do you identify with most and why?

4. After reading about these women, what is the unifying theme throughout the Bible?

5. Each of the women had unique gifts used by God. What are your gifts?

Did you know?

The Resurrection can be proven through the 1 Corinthians 15 creed which claims that Christ died, was buried, was raised after three days, and appeared to more than 500 people. This passage is one of the earliest and best-authenticated passages, dated approximately two years after Jesus' death, thus proving that the eyewitnesses could not have made false claims. Jesus' burial is also one of the earliest and best-attested facts that we have about the Resurrection. In all four gospels, Joseph of Arimathea, an anti-Christian Jewish leader, is the person who gave Jesus an honorable burial. If this was a legend, then the authors would not have wanted to invent the name of someone who had condemned Jesus. The security of the tomb and the discovery made by women finding it empty also give evidence against fabricating a lie. (Strobel 2016, 249-152)

What will you do to pass on the message?

ACKNOWLEDGMENTS

Above all, I want to thank my mother, the Rev. Jasmin Hivale, whom I grew up watching her write long sermons on her bed as I mothered my dolls. She is my encourager and inspiration and without her I would never have met the chosen women in the Bible.

Thank you to my husband Jim, who chose me. He is my love, my rock, my pillar, and without him I wouldn't be a mother.

Thank you to my sister friends; you know who you are. The ones who have shared deep conversations, struggled through difficult times, laughed till our stomachs hurt, and even from a distance could still pick up where we left off. You are my chosen women.

Finally thank you to my daughters, Jayani and Kylie, whom God chose for me to pass on the message of hope. I love you the greenest.

I love you the Greenest

"Mama, who do you love most?"
I love you the bluest.
I love you like a mother gazing at her newborn's navy eyes
the color of crisp snow before the morning sun finds it
a burst of fireworks lighting up a New Year's night sky
the brilliance of sapphire ice
the radiance of the sparkling winter sea
the warmth of a cozy baby sweater.

"Mama, who do you love most?"
I love you the yellowest.
I love you like a mother in awe of her babies' golden locks
the color of spring sun warming the sandy beaches
a young chick cracking away her shell
refreshing lemonade
a shiny rare jade
the softness of a daffodil.

And when they were finally asleep
she wrapped in her lonely mint shawl
and dreamed of leaping frogs on mossy rocks
two girls dancing in the grass
in lime summer dresses
under the swaying trees.

Dedicated to my daughters while their father served in Afghanistan.
(Adapted from the story "I love you the Purplest" by Barbara Joosse)

BIBLIOGRAPHY

Bruce, F.F. (1956) 2006. *Second Thoughts on the Dead Sea Scrolls.* Eugene, OR: Wipf & Stock Pub.

"Genesis - What Is the Significance of Seal, Cord, and Staff?" n.d. Biblical Hermeneutics Stack Exchange. Accessed March 27, 2021. https://hermeneutics.stackexchange.com/questions/13028/what-is-the-significance-of-seal-cord-and-staff.

Kaiser Jr., Walter. C., and Duane Garrett. (2005) 2010. *NIV Archaeological Study Bible: An Illustrated Walk through Biblical History and Culture.* Grand Rapids, MI: Zondervan.

NIV Bible in 90 Days: Cover to Cover in 12 Pages a Day. 2012. Grand Rapids, MI: Zondervan.

Strobel, Lee. (1998) 2016. *The Case for Christ.* Grand Rapids, MI: Zondervan.

———. 2010. *The Case for Christ Study Bible: Investigating the Evidence for Belief.* Grand Rapids, MI: Zondervan.

———. (2010) 2014. *The Case for Faith: A Journalist Investigates the Toughest Objections to Christianity.* Grand Rapids, MI: Zondervan.

The Flood. 2019. "The Flood." Answers in Genesis. 2019. https://answersingenesis.org/the-flood/.

CPSIA information can be obtained
at www.ICGtesting.com
Printed in the USA
BVHW052033240821
615132BV00015BA/658